Choosing and Using Music in Training

Choosing and Using Music in Training

Liz Brant and Tony Harvey

Gower

Published by
Gower Publishing Limited
Gower House
Croft Road
Aldershot
Hants GU11 3HR
England

Gower Publishing Company
131 Main Street
Burlington VT 05401-5600 USA

British Library Cataloguing in Publication Data
Brant, Liz
    Choosing and using music in training
    1. Music in education   2. Employees – Training of
    I. Title   II. Harvey, Tony
    658.3'124

    ISBN 0 566 08426 0

Library of Congress Card Number: 2001086889

Typeset by Wileman Design.
Printed and bound in Great Britain by
Antony Rowe Ltd., Chippenham, Wiltshire.

Contents

Acknowledgements

We would like to acknowledge two people whose ideas inspired us to put together this CD and book. Thank you to Elizabeth Miles for her incredibly detailed book on using music to manage your mind, body and mood, and to Colin Rose for his excellent book on Accelerated Learning.

LB and TH

1 Introduction

This is a book for trainers. It is about using music in learning environments, such as training courses. It has been written to help trainers who want to use music to support the learning process but who may not know where to start, who want more background information before they do or who want to reduce the risk of using music and getting it all wrong. It will also be of use to trainers who have been using music for a while and who want to achieve more.

Accompanying the book is a compilation of music suited to various circumstances and desired learning states. This compilation will act as a good general starter kit for trainers using music.

As a starting point, think about the suitability of music for different situations. Decide which types of music you would like to hear for each of the following scenarios:

Situation	Beat			Volume		
1 A step class at the gym	Fast ☐	Medium ☐	Slow ☐	High ☐	Medium ☐	Low ☐
2 The opening to *Match of the Day*	Fast ☐	Medium ☐	Slow ☐	High ☐	Medium ☐	Low ☐
3 Film soundtrack for a Merchant Ivory film set in Tuscany	Fast ☐	Medium ☐	Slow ☐	High ☐	Medium ☐	Low ☐
4 In a nightclub	Fast ☐	Medium ☐	Slow ☐	High ☐	Medium ☐	Low ☐
5 Driving home after a tough workout in the gym	Fast ☐	Medium ☐	Slow ☐	High ☐	Medium ☐	Low ☐
6 Driving fast on an open road with the roof down	Fast ☐	Medium ☐	Slow ☐	High ☐	Medium ☐	Low ☐
7 Doing the weekly grocery shop at the supermarket	Fast ☐	Medium ☐	Slow ☐	High ☐	Medium ☐	Low ☐
8 Film soundtrack for a moving and emotional scene	Fast ☐	Medium ☐	Slow ☐	High ☐	Medium ☐	Low ☐
9 Music played on a telephone waiting system	Fast ☐	Medium ☐	Slow ☐	High ☐	Medium ☐	Low ☐
10 Boxers entering the ring in a big prize fight	Fast ☐	Medium ☐	Slow ☐	High ☐	Medium ☐	Low ☐

Although most of us will have responded in similar ways to each of the ten situations, clearly our musical preferences can change according to the activity we are doing. The following pages will explain why this happens.

2 Background

Over the last 30 years there has been increasing interest in the use of music in learning environments. It is not unusual for a trainer to include a small audio unit and a stack of music CDs in the equipment for a training course, and for music to be played at certain key times throughout a training event.

Trainers are using music to create a welcoming atmosphere for nervous participants, to help learners reflect, to give people energy boosts and to encourage creativity.

The soothing and life-giving effects of music have been recognized since ancient times. The list of those who have advocated using music to change mood and promote well-being reads like a *Who's Who* of civilization since written records began.

Confucius, Aristotle, Homer, Plato, Pythagorus, St Augustine, shamans of Central Russia and Indian mystics all used music in their daily lives. And not just any music. The ancient Greeks recognized that music should be carefully selected to get the desired outcome; they chanted to music played at the pace and rhythm of the human heart. Music and rhythm has been used consistently throughout history to fire up soldiers for battle, as indeed the All Blacks use the *haka* to fire themselves up for a rugby match. Music has also been the tool of shamans and mystics to induce planned states of mind and body and to relieve pain. According to Colin Rose in his book, *Accelerated Learning*, ancient Tamil literature talks of music being used to help crops grow. In the twentieth century the pioneering work of Dr Georgi Lozanov of the University of Sophia in Bulgaria showed that music enhances learning.

In February 1996 *Newsweek* magazine reported various research studies that discussed the benefits of using music in teaching children. The so-called 'Mozart Effect' appears to show a link between children listening to Mozart and the strengthening of their neuro circuits used for mathematics.

Focus now on your own response to music and look back at the replies you gave to the questions in the Introduction. You probably chose medium to fast beat and high volume music for the nightclub. Just suppose that the nightclub music changed from loud and funky to soft and classical. How would this make you feel and how would it change the mood in the club?

Clearly music does have an impact on how we feel, think and act. But why should this be and what can our natural preferences show us about how to use music to create effective learning environments?

3 The Theory

For years scientists have sought to explain why external sounds and rhythms affect the human body.

In the early 1800s psychologists were using music to alter a patient's state of mind. They first matched a depressed state of mind with downbeat music and then gradually quickened the pace and tempo until the patient's state of mind matched the desired state. Professional boxing uses a similar technique. A blast of loud music with a strong, repetitive beat signals the arrival of the boxers in the ring and primes the audience to start to feel the tension and excitement.

So what can science tell us? It all hinges on electricity and brain-waves. Brain-waves indicate the electrical activity in the brain. When we are feeling relaxed our brain-waves are slower and when we are feeling energized our brain-waves are faster.

If our minds are racing and we are feeling fidgety we are likely to find quiet focused work difficult or impossible. Conversely, if we were feeling chilled out and mellow, to switch into thinking creatively would not be easy. Brain-waves determine how effective we are at doing a particular task and brain-waves can be altered by music.

There are four types of brain-wave: alpha, beta, theta and delta. Brain-waves are measured in cycles per second.

When we experience:

alpha brain-waves
- we are relaxed but still alert
- thought processes will be clear and calm
- concentration will be focused
- the brain is open to new information
- the rate is approximately 8–13 cycles per second.

beta brain-waves
- we are alert and very able to use our critical minds to make decisions and solve immediate problems
- many thoughts can be handled at once
- the rate is approximately 13–30 cycles per second.

theta brain-waves
- we are being creative and are able to use our imagination
- we are able to see things from novel perspectives
- these brain-waves can also indicate stress
- the rate is approximately 4–9 cycles per second.

delta brain-waves
- we are in deep sleep
- the rate is less than 6 cycles per second.

4 How Music Can Change Our Physiology

In the same way that nineteenth-century psychologists used music to change a person's state of mind, so we can use music to alter their brainwaves and this has a knock-on effect on the person's physiology.

When sound enters the human ear it is converted by the cochlea into electrical impulses that pass to the brain. Different music will have different effects. Soft or loud music, music we know well versus music that is unknown to us, music that is played on one instrument contrasted with music played by an orchestra; our responses to each will vary.

As the ancient Greeks knew, and science as we know it has confirmed, music affects our psychophysiology. That is, it affects our minds (both our emotions and our logical thought processes) and it affects our physiology. We can expect to experience certain physiological changes according to which piece of music is being played.

Autonomic responses

So which parts of our bodies does music affect? Music affects our autonomic system responses, which means that our breathing, blood pressure, pulse rate and the electrical activities of muscles are all affected by what we hear.

Fast, rhythmic music gets us 'going'. Our beta brain-waves increase, our heart, pulse and rate of breathing go up, our blood pressure increases, our ability to take in a lot of external information and make quick decisions goes up, we become more co-ordinated and there is increased electrical activity in our muscles. And, if the volume is pumped up, more electrical impulses per second are sent to the brain. Loud, rhythmic music is literally electrifying.

By contrast, quiet, slow, soft music decreases our autonomic responses. Pulse rate and breathing also change to match the beat of the music. Less electricity reaches our muscles and we feel more relaxed and calm.

Research shows that responses to music are fairly universal. Music that matches the beat of the human heart (around 80 beats per minute) appears to be the most comfortable across cultures.

Responses are of course individualized, so that if we do not like a piece of loud, rhythmic music our autonomic response to it may be low. In addition, music can be evocative of strong memories. If the memory is not a positive one it is that which clouds the mind. This will work against the effect you are setting out to achieve as a trainer and we will talk more about this later.

Finally, actually hearing the music is not necessary. Someone with hearing difficulties can still experience physiological changes to music. Evelyn Glennie, the world-renowned percussionist, who has been profoundly deaf since the age of 12, does not hear the amazing sounds she can get from her percussion instruments, nor the sounds of the orchestra she is playing with, but she can feel the vibrations through her hands and feet, and the whole of her body.

5 More About The Human Brain

The ancient Egyptians considered that there was great significance in the two sides of the human brain. They had noticed that an injury to one side of the brain led to paralysis in the opposite side of the body.

Specialization in the brain – myth or fact?

Today, our knowledge of brain function is developing all the time. In the 1960s the pioneering work of Nobel Prize winners Roger Sperry and Robert Ornstein pointed to specialization in brain function by the two hemispheres, giving us the traditional paradigm of the left brain being analytical and logical and the right brain being more creative and emotional.

This paradigm continues to hold some credibility but more recent research suggests that the separate components of a function, for example speaking or being creative, are carried out by the two hemispheres of the brain working differently but in unison. Susan Greenfield, in her fascinating book and BBC2 TV series *Brain Story*, gives the example of someone suffering damage to the right hemisphere of their brain being able to communicate verbally but in a toneless voice because the damage to their right hemisphere means they are unable to convey emotion. In summary, the two hemispheres work together to give us the ability to operate in a multi-dimensional way. So to be creative we need technique and detail from our left hemisphere and flow and emotion from our right hemisphere.

Our appreciation of music depends on our right hemisphere processing melodies and harmonies and our left hemisphere processing rhythm and lyrics. Of the two sides of the brain – in most people – the right side is typically the more dominant in music processing.

Susan Greenfield, however, quotes a recent study of university students who were about to start a three-year course in music. All were put through a standard test for checking which side of the brain was dominant for music. At the start of their course they predictably showed right brain dominance but the same test carried out at the end of the three years showed left brain dominance. Her conclusion is that the students' studies forced them to start processing music in a more analytical way. So left and right brain dominance can shift.

Today, writers on brain function talk more confidently about generalities and tendencies and less about absolutes. Current thinking is well represented by Greenfield's statement that: 'the difference between the left and right hemispheres is one of degree rather than of absolute distinction ... This habit of matching function to lobe is an old one in neuroscience ...'.

So how do the two sides of the brain communicate with each other and produce integrated thought? The two sides of the brain are linked by a bundle of nerves called the *corpus callosum* – our white matter as opposed to our grey matter. The *corpus callosum* allows for exchange of information between the two sides of the brain and is often likened to a superhighway. This important bundle of nerves is thicker in women than in men and research indicates that adults who learned how to play a musical instrument as a child have a larger than average *corpus callosum*. The larger this superhighway is, the more information is being exchanged and the more we access both hemispheres, the more intelligently we are able to function. Indeed there are strong arguments for moving away from traditional schooling in only the three R's of 'reading, 'riting and 'rithmetic' which use a high percentage of left brain function.

Research in the United States shows that where there is a combination of both left- and right-brained subjects (that is, including art, music and drama) in the curriculum, performance improves in subjects where the left brain is used more. Further evidence suggests that learning to play a musical instrument is associated with an improvement in spatial ability. Anecdotal evidence indicates that when Mozart is played to children the right side of the brain is stimulated and their mathematical ability improves.

Genius ...

It seems that when individuals are able to use both sides of their brains, they are capable of great creativity and, in some cases, real genius. Einstein is often quoted as an example. As a scientist he excelled in logic and analysis yet his ideas came to him first in pictures. Likewise, Leonardo da Vinci was a scientist and an artist.

Back to our ancestors ...

It is not actually surprising that how we feel and what we do should be linked to what we hear.

The first sensory organ to develop in the womb is the ear. Even in the womb we are able to hear sounds from the outside world, so that newborn babies recognize their parents' voices. Hearing is our primary defence mechanism. Our cave-living ancestors would have relied on their hearing to protect them from hungry predators. On identifying the sound of an approaching sabre-toothed tiger, the cave man would have felt fear and his brain would have alerted his body to run or fight. So it is today that our hearing, our emotions and our actions are closely connected and music can induce in us both positive and negative emotions.

6 Types Of Music

Earlier this century Georgi Lozanov, working at the University of Sophia in Bulgaria, pioneered the use of classical music to accelerate learning. Lozanov wanted to create a mood of calm and relaxed alertness that we now know to be caused by alpha brain-waves. The ideal music to achieve this was baroque music and particularly pieces composed between 1700–1750. Baroque composers aimed to free the mind from day-to-day concerns and the music they composed had an unusually precise rhythm that is just a little slower than the number of beats per minute of the human heart. He found that each piece tended to end on a bright and refreshing note. Bach, Vivaldi and Handel are particularly effective.

In training we use the full range of music that is on the market, from baroque to modern classical, jazz, reggae, pop, blues, cartoon and film sound-tracks, salsa, steel bands, choral works, big bands, drums, opera, Gregorian chants, symphonies, acoustic strings, rock, punk, rap, wind instruments, solo piano, sounds of nature (rainforest, surf, and so on) and the many types of indigenous music which often appear on world music compilations.

Trust your own intuition. If you hear a piece of music that you think is appropriate, use it, and assess the value for yourself.

7 Other Factors That Will Determine How Music Will Affect Us

There are many factors that will determine how effective a piece of music will be in giving us the outcome we want. Elizabeth Miles, in her excellent book, *Tune Your Brain: using music to manage your mind, body and mood*, explores these factors in great detail.

Obscure, slow music with an unpredictable rhythm will have a different effect to a slow, well-known piece with a steady rhythm. Similarly, highly rhythmic music with lyrics will have a different effect to rhythmic music with no lyrics.

The main factors that affect the outcome of music are:

- Speed – the beats per minute of the music: fast, slow, moderate
- Volume
- Rhythm
- Instrumentation – one instrument or an orchestra
- The listeners' familiarity with the piece of music
- Whether the piece of music is actually liked or not
- Whether participants accept the use of music or not
- Whether the music is with or without lyrics.

Speed

The human heart beats at an average rate of 80 beats per minute. If a piece of music is faster our autonomic responses will increase and if the beat of the music is slower our autonomic responses will decrease. Ultimately we might fall asleep just as a baby might to the smooth sound of a lullaby.

Volume

As sound enters the ear it is converted into electrical impulses and the louder the volume the more electricity is generated.

Rhythm

Predictable rhythms are easy to focus on, especially if there are no lyrics. This is often music that we don't really listen to and it is very good for reflection and for carrying out monotonous tasks.

Varied and unfamiliar rhythms create new neural networks and are good for creativity.

Instrumentation

Solo instruments work well for promoting relaxation and unfamiliar sounds again excite the brain and are good for creativity. World music is particularly good for this as it combines native traditional instruments such as panpipes or didgeridoos with classical western ones.

Familiarity

If the music is familiar as well as clear and uncluttered it can be good for relaxation and reflection.

However, music can be a great memory trigger and the listeners' minds might get flooded in memories that prevent them achieving the task in hand.

Listener preference

If we dislike a piece of music it is not likely to give us the outcome we want. Watch out for signs that participants do not like the track you are playing and switch tracks immediately.

Listener acceptance

Listening to music in a learning environment can seem odd to some people, particularly if they have traditional expectations of the training event. Experience tells us that most people grow to like it. It is important to explain to people why you are using music itself and why you are using particular styles of music. Playing music in breaks helps people become used to hearing it and can create a good relaxing or 'welcome back' response.

Remember, we are all sophisticated users of sound stimulation to change or maintain our moods! We listen to morning radio shows and 'drive time' radio shows, both of which tend to use beta beat music. We also listen to silence to clear our minds. Using music in the training room is therefore an extension of what people do in their everyday lives.

Clearly if participants object to the music it would

be better to remove the barrier to learning and switch it off, than to persist in trying to persuade people to change their mind.

With or without lyrics?

Words can be a distraction and in most training situations we would advise the use of music without lyrics. Certain exceptions would be where:

- the lyrics are murmured, as in some Enya works
- the lyrics are in an obscure language and the voice effectively becomes an instrument
- the piece of music is particularly evocative of strong positive memories
- the lyrics themselves are relevant, as with 'We Are The Champions', although this is a rather overused track and has become a cliché.

8 How Trainers Use Music

As trainers we need to be able to be able to do a variety of things, such as:

- create a welcoming atmosphere in the training room
- help participants be creative
- help everyone keep energized
- encourage reflection
- send everyone off on a positive note
- make sure our own brain-waves are the most effective for what WE want to do.

We will look at each scenario, assess the ideal brain-wave frequency required and then consider the characteristics of the music we might choose to play.

Create a welcoming atmosphere in the training room

Participants may feel nervous at the start of a training event. As trainers we need them to feel as relaxed as possible and also be focused on the purpose of the training and the material we are going to cover. The ideal brain-wave frequency will be beta.

We will want to get off to a good start. In our experience it is best to avoid a well-known piece of music just in case the memories it triggers are negative. Try a piece of music that is upbeat with a mix of the known and the unknown (world music is ideal) and make sure the volume is high enough for the music to fill the room but not too loud as to be uncomfortable. Always have the music playing as participants come into the room. If you are unsure when that will be, set the CD player to continually repeat the track before going to meet your participants.

Help participants be creative

There are certain times during a course when you want participants to be creative and move away from conventional ways of thinking. The ideal brain-wave frequency for creativity is theta.

Creativity is helped by music that is made of complex sounds and that has contrasting and varied beats. World music can be ideal again as unfamiliar sounds create new neural networks and greater neurological excitement and can nudge participants into new ways of thinking. Keep the volume moderate to low. Again it is best to choose lyric-free music.

Help everyone keep energized

At certain key points during the day you might notice the energy levels fall and participants might be in danger of dropping off to sleep, especially in a large course group. In order to maintain focus and concentration you will need to raise the brain-wave frequency to alpha or beta.

If you are some way into the course you might use

a well-known, upbeat track with lyrics (watch for any negative reactions as memories are triggered). Lyrics are usually acceptable in music used to energize. Strong rhythms, such as sambas, work well. Surprising and unexpected blasts of trumpets are great, big bands are terrific – and remember to pump up the volume.

Encourage reflection

From David Kolb's work on the learning cycle (see *Experiential Learning*) we know that in order to learn most effectively your participants will need to reflect on what they have done or what they are currently doing. Alpha brain-waves are ideal for quiet reflection. Use music that has a slow, even tempo and a regular rhythm. Turn the volume down low.

If you want participants to focus on a reflective individual task, say completing a questionnaire, use music with a simple, predictable rhythm and familiar sounds and absolutely no lyrics.

Send everyone off on a positive note

At the end of the course you want all participants to leave feeling optimistic and good about themselves. Beta brain-waves are ideal for this.

Broadly speaking, play the same music as you would for energizers and if you find a lyric with meaning all the better. In the same way that course groups develop a group language you might have a group CD track that you will play them out to.

Finally, with music to send people off, use the repeat button so the track keeps playing until everyone has left the room.

Make sure your own brain-waves are the most effective for what YOU want to do

Use the same principles in your own personal use of music. For quiet preparation on the morning the course is due to start, play music at low volume to focus your attention. Just before you open the course play a track that triggers memories of success. When participants have left the room at the end of the day play some low-volume, chill out music.

9 Not Forgetting Silence!

If music can affect mood positively so can silence. An environment in which music figures significantly can be enhanced by not using music. That silence can then give sound real impact later!

10 Equipment To Use

For most applications a portable CD/cassette player is most effective. However, one should be chosen that provides the following functions:

- A high power output is necessary. This is not so much to be able to play music very loud but to be able to fill a room with music without distorting it. For similar reasons, the machine should have a strong bass response. The best type will have a bass boost and bass reflex speakers. This prevents the music sounding thin or 'tinny'.

- The start, pause and stop controls should be separate, large and easily accessible buttons. These are the most commonly used controls and often need to be found quickly.

- Fast forward and fast reverse may be useful if you want to find a portion of a track. If this is the case you may want to cue the portion with either a timer or counter read-out or using a set of earphones.

- Controls to step forward or back track by track are essential, to help you locate the track you want. Even better would be a keypad, used to enter the track number you want.

- A large volume control that allows fine, slow and continuous adjustment of volume, both up and down, is much preferable to a slider control that can sound jerky when used.

- The machine should have a setting that allows 'single track', 'continuous' or 'track repeat' play. This provides different combinations so that you can play one track and then stop, play CD tracks in sequence or repeatedly play the same track. Random play may be of some use if all the tracks create similar responses but otherwise it introduces an element of unnecessary risk of disruption.

A cassette play option can be useful for odd tracks and for using audiotapes for other purposes. In general though it would be better to use CDs.

For larger training or conference rooms, you may need to use a PA (public address system). These may come with remote controls or, for conference-type events, you may have an assistant to work with you. You should become familiar with the control unit used or, if using an assistant, brief the assistant very clearly indeed.

11 Legality And Licensing

Unless you write and record all the music you use yourself, the music you play will be the intellectual property of one or more other parties. The rights of the property owners are protected in the UK by the Copyright Designs and Patents Act (1988).

As such you may not play music in public without being licensed. It is not sufficient to have bought the CD or tape. That only gives you the right to play the music in private. A public event is any event other than a family or domestic gathering. Therefore, any training course, whether paid for or not, for commercial gain or not, is a public event. There is no way round this. The law makes no distinction between the status of the learners, the status of the trainers or the type of organization – private enterprise, public authority or voluntary body.

There are two licences required before you can legally play music in public. The licences are issued by two different organizations, the contact details of which are included at the end of this chapter.

The first licence is issued by the Performing Rights Society (PRS). The PRS licence covers the premises where the music is played. The proceeds are distributed to composers and music publishers. A PRS licence is necessary for the playing of live, broadcast and pre-recorded music.

The second licence is issued by Phonographic

Performance Limited (PPL). PPL licences cover the use of sound recordings. The proceeds are distributed to record companies, recording artists and musicians.

PPL licences are usually held by the occupier of the premises where the music is played. However, all parties involved in the use of the recordings have equal responsibility under law. If you rent equipment or recordings, the supplier will normally have to obtain a PPL licence. If you run training courses at your employer's own venues your employer will normally be the licensed authority. If you work for a training provider, the provider must be licensed. If you are an independent trainer, that means you must obtain your own licence. If you use other venues, you should check that the venue also holds a PRS licence.

A PPL licence will state the exact terms and conditions for its use. The appropriate category for using music in the way we have indicated is 'Background Music'. The appropriate form is GLD06 and the appropriate tariff is Tariff 018 (Background Music – Miscellaneous Tariff). In your application you should state that you will be using recorded music as background music in various premises (state whether the premises are owned by you or not, or a combination) and on various equipment (state whether the equipment is owned by you or not, or a combination). You may only use recorded music within the terms and conditions set on the licence as issued. You may not copy it or re-record it. PPL will be able to advise you if you have any special requirements. If you use recorded music in a more prominent way, for example if you are running music workshops or dance lessons, you will need a different category of licence.

Using music without the correct licence is theft. It deprives the owners of the intellectual property of proceeds that is legally theirs. There are an increasing number of cases of unlicensed users being taken to court. Courts have the power to stop you from using recorded music and to fine you for damages and costs.

Contact details

Performing Rights Society
 29-33 Berners Street
 London
 W1P 4AA
 Tel : 020 7580 5544
 Fax : 020 7306 4455
 http://www.prs.co.uk

Phonographic Performance Ltd
 1 Upper James Street
 London
 W1R 3HG
 Tel : 020 7534 1000
 Fax : 020 7534 1111

12 Frequently Asked Questions

Q1   Can I use only music that is free from copyright?

A   This question comes about because the term of copyright is 70 years from the death of the author of the work. Many trainers believe that as a consequence they can play recordings of baroque and older classical music without a licence. But this belief takes no account of the rights of the publisher and other parties involved. You can use any recorded music if you have a PRS licence and a PPL licence. See Chapter 11 on Legality and Licensing.

Q2   I am not running training courses for profit. Do I still need a licence?

A   Yes, in every case you will need a PRS licence and, if playing recorded music, a PPL licence. This also applies to voluntary organizations and charities.

Q3   How long should I play music for?

A   This depends on what you are using music for. If for example you are using it for background music while syndicate groups work on a case study, play it for the duration of an exercise and turn it down very low, or turn it off, for the discussion that follows.

Q4   How loud should I play the music?

A   We mostly use music in training rooms as background music to stimulate effective brain-waves and not to entertain. Generally, therefore, keep the volume audible and low. Exceptions to this are when you are using music as an energizer or when you are using it personally to psyche yourself up. Energizing music can be played at a higher volume. Take your cue from your participants as to how loud that should be. When you use music to prepare yourself before participants arrive, remember that by pumping up the volume you increase electricity in your body and literally fire yourself up.

Q5   Should I play only classical music?

A   We play the full range of music on the market. Use classical music and contemporary music.

Q6   How should I deal with participants' requests for particular music, especially when it is unsuitable?

A   We address this by first explaining why we use music and then the different effects different types of music have on our behaviour. We then ask people to select music that suits the current purpose. Involving people in this way clearly has many benefits. If some people then still ask for unsuitable music from particular artists and bands, we defer playing that music to a social time and reinforce our reasoning.

Q7 When should I play music?

A   We regularly use music when:
- people enter the training room (welcoming music)
- people are working on exercises (reflecting and creativity music)
- peoples' energy levels are low (energizing music)
- we want people to reflect and review (reflecting music)
- we want people to depart in a positive frame of mind (departing music).

We sometimes play music that stimulates alpha waves, such as baroque music, very quietly behind a trainer-led plenary discussion. With a group that acknowledges the value of music we have found this can help people concentrate.

Q8 What do I do if some people in the room like music and others don't?

A   This is a matter of judgement, based upon your clarity about what you are trying to achieve. It could be that someone dislikes the track you are playing rather than music in general. First explain why music is being used and offer an alternative track. If someone was still unhappy with music being played we would suggest you turn it off but perhaps play it in breaks on low volume.

Q9   Are there some people who do not benefit from music being played?

A   In our experience if someone is played a piece of music that they find pleasing and/or interesting, it will have a beneficial effect. Benefit is achieved by carefully choosing appropriate music. We know that sound, in this case music, alters brain-waves and we know that brain-waves determine how effective we are at completing certain tasks. We sometimes come across people who associate music with distraction or background, such as the 'muzak' played in supermarkets and other shops. Once people accept and experience the use of appropriate music in training we find that everyone benefits.

Q10   Do I still need to be licensed even though I have bought this CD and book?

A   Yes!

13 In Conclusion

We have explored with you the historic background to using music in daily life. When on the way to the office you tune into your favourite 'drive time' show featuring foot tapping, upbeat tracks you are doing what your ancestors have done for thousands of years – matching music to suit your mood.

We have looked at how music affects our psychophysiology and we have explored the connection between music and brain-waves. We also looked at how listening to music appears to increase the size of our *corpus callosum*, allowing for greater flow of information between the two hemispheres, so improving the integration of right- and left-brain activity and contributing to overall improved performance.

We then looked at how trainers can use music to enhance learning by carefully matching the type of music to the mood they want to create. We outlined the equipment you need to maximize the impact of any music you play and we finally gave you full details of how to ensure that you are on the right side of the law when you use music as part of your training.

We are confident that you will be delighted by the eclectic mix of tracks on the accompanying CD.

And finally, taking a line from the immortals of Eurorock, Abba, we would like to express our gratitude to those towers of talent that made this all possible and say 'Thank you for the music'!

14 The Playlist

Track Name	Time	Composer/Origin	Welcoming	Creativity	Energizing	Reflecting	Departing
Welcoming							
Horn Concerto No. 3	3'20	Mozart	◆				◇
Straw Hat	2'00	West Indies	◆		◇		
Arrival of the Queen of Sheba	2'20	Handel	◆				
Piano Concerto No. 23 – Presto	7'49	Mozart	◆		◇		
Creativity							
Brandenburg Concerto 1 Allegro	4'25	Bach	◇	◆			
O'er the Moor	3'01	Ireland	◇	◆		◇	
Monsoon Evening	2'24	India		◆			
The March of Brian Boru	2'01	The Chieftains		◆			
Energizing							
Takirari	2'22	South America			◆		◇
Happy Whistlers	1'30	Cartoon		◇	◆		
Entry of the Gladiators	2'40	Mechanical Organ			◆		
Behind the Beat	3'19	Africa			◆		

Track Name	Time	Composer/Origin	Welcoming	Creativity	Energizing	Reflecting	Departing
Reflecting							
Piano Concerto No. 21 – Andante	7'02	Mozart	◇			◆	
Moonlight Sonata – Adagio	4'11	Beethoven	◇			◆	
Celestial Dancer	2'28	Burma	◇			◆	
Beyond the Ganges	1'27	SE Asia				◆	
Departing							
Liberty Bell – theme tune from Monty Python	3'35	USA March			◇		◆
La La Lo	3'29	Salsa			◇		◆
Cat Boogie	2'16	Piano			◇		◆
Royal Pavilion 2	3'16	Classical Guitar	◇		◇		◆

Note

The table above gives all the tracks at a glance. We give the track times, but remember if the track time is too short just put your CD player on to repeat or work your way through all the tracks for the particular use you want. The table also indicates how the tracks can be used. Primary use is indicated by a solid diamond ◆ and secondary use by an open diamond ◇. However, some of the welcoming tracks can be used for energizing and departing and vice versa, and if you want to start your course with something mellow and soothing try using some of the reflecting tracks. Have fun and try out the tracks for yourselves to work out the best fit for the type of training you are doing.

Bibliography And Further Reading

Greenfield, Susan (2000), *Brain Story*, BBC publications: London.

Kolb, D. A. et al (1984), *Experiential Learning*, Prentice Hall: London.

Miles, Elizabeth (1997), *Tune Your Brain: using music to manage your mind, body and mood*, Berkley: CA.

Moir, Anne and Jessel, David (1989), *Brain Sex*, Mandarin Publications: London.

Rose, Colin (1996), *Accelerated Learning*, Accelerated Learning Systems Limited: UK.

Russell, Peter (1979), *The Brain Book*, Routledge and Kegan Paul: London.

'Your Child's Brain' (February 1996), *Newsweek* magazine: New York.